Rejection Proof Therapy 101

How to Overcome, Deal With and Heal Yourself from Rejection

By Madison Taylor

Table of Contents

.

Introduction

Everyone can agree that rejection sucks. Rejection makes you question your self-esteem and your abilities. It makes you feel like you are not good enough. The pain of rejection can certainly crush your ego and hurt you to your core.

Humans are naturally social beings. We all want to feel accepted and loved. Rejection is an affront to our need to be accepted. Being told that we are not good enough means that we are not an accepted part of the herd, and that triggers deep fear and pain within our hearts. The horrible hurt that rejection can cause us creates a deep-seated fear of rejection in many people.

Sadly, many people are ruled by their fear of rejection. They erect safe little boxes of limitation around themselves and never take the risks necessary to start a business or approach a pretty woman. Their lives become very limited and they miss out on potentially great things because of their fear. Fear of rejection has a powerful way of making people avoid taking important risks and missing out on life. Living this way is a shame. You are missing out on potential acceptance by staying in a safety box and trying to escape rejection. Just because rejection sucks does not mean that you should limit yourself in life to avoid it.

Like all fears, a fear of rejection is something that you need to conquer. Exposing yourself to rejection is one way to overcome the fear of it. Working to look at rejection as a growing experience, rather than a hurtful experience, can also help condition you to face rejection without fear because you begin to see that it is really nothing to be afraid of.

It is not possible to truly be rejection-proof. Rejection happens and is an inevitable part of life. You cannot become immune to rejection. Rather, it is best to accept that rejection will happen to you during your lifetime, probably many times. It cannot be avoided or entirely prevented, no matter how hard you try.

But you can improve your chances of getting a yes. The way you present yourself to the world and the way you drive negotiations or flirt with people you like can influence your success in life. You are less likely to be rejected if you use certain methods of approaching others, such as exuding confidence and selling yourself without modesty. If you make others feel like what you offer them is too good to pass up, then you will get a yes.

You can also change how you think about rejection. If you remove the fear and the horribleness of rejection from your mind, then rejection is no longer so scary. You can actually use rejection to your advantage. Rejection provides you a chance to grow as a person and to improve what you have to offer business partners or romantic prospects. If you can change how you feel about rejection and how you view it, you can remove the fear of it. Without a fear of rejection, you will no longer be too afraid to strike out and try to accomplish new things.

Fear can be decimated when you stop taking rejection personally. It can also be decimated when you stop giving it power over you. You can accept that rejection hurts, but you do not need to let that fear of pain dictate how you live. Instead, embrace rejection as a natural part of life and refuse to give it any power or influence over your decisions.

This is what it really means to be rejection-proof. If you wear a bullet-proof vest, you have just as much likelihood to be shot at as without a vest on. But the bullets bounce off of you and do not puncture your skin. It is the same idea with being rejection-proof. Rejection is still a possibility. But rejection will bounce off of you and you will be able to move on without the ego destruction that rejection can cause some people. Rejection will no longer kill your ego.

This book is your ultimate guide to becoming rejection-proof. You will learn how to view rejection differently so that you can handle it in a more helpful manner. You also will learn to lower your chances of being rejected and increase your chances of being accepted. Rejection will no longer be able to get to you once you apply the concepts included in this book. As a result, you can start to tackle things in life that you never imagined doing before. You will be more willing to take on great risks because you are not afraid of the consequences. By taking these risks, you may end up turning

your life into something greater than you ever
imagined.

Chapter 1: Why Rejection Hurts

It is no secret that rejection hurts. But why does rejection cause people such severe pain? Rejection hurts so much that people often cringe away from it the way they would cringe away from a hot burner or a torture device. People shy away from the pain naturally, indicating that people are instinctively programmed to not want to experience rejection.

When you experience rejection, the pain centers of your brain activate. The same neurons that light up when you break a leg light up when you are rejected. Basically, your brain experiences the same sensations as physical pain when you are faced with rejection. Scientists who put subjects under MRI machines and then asked the subjects to recall a recent rejection saw the same neural activity in the brain as in the brains of people suffering physical pain.

The pain of rejection is very severe and very real. You feel it throughout your body. Even a small friendship falling apart or a group of strangers snubbing you at a club can create a crippling sense of rejection.

On top of feeling rejected, you also probably feel ashamed of how hurt you are. You do not want to admit that something so small was able to make you hurt so much. It is possible that you do not even understand why even the smallest rejections hurt. You can feel more vulnerable with a small rejection because you wonder how badly a severe rejection will hurt.

Then, if you do experience a true severe rejection, you feel so terrible that you are unable to function. You may feel like you have lost someone dear to you and you may feel that you have lost a part of yourself. Rejection by your family or even society as a whole can cause you truly crippling pain. The blow to your ego is on par with a bad blow to your body.

The human brain treats rejection with the same severity as a serious physical injury because the human brain is hardwired to rely on the acceptance of others. Being accepted by other human beings is just as important to the brain as preserving your physical health and bodily wellness. This neural response to rejection is a residual effect from the hunter-gatherer days of human history, when humans had to stick together for survival. Being a part of the herd meant that your chances of survival were higher because you had others help you sense and defend yourself against danger. Not being a part of the herd meant that you had to fend for yourself, and you likely could not last long spotting and fending off danger all by yourself. In the scary caveman days, all sorts of dangers existed, from wild animals to natural catastrophes. Taking care of yourself in caveman times was nearly impossible without teamwork.

The human brain thus became hardwired to sense rejection with the same terror as a physical attack on the body. When the brain senses rejection, it is programmed to respond immediately with intense discomfort. This discomfort is designed to make humans adjust their behavior in order to be accepted as part of the herd, to increase their chances of survival. This is why people are so determined to conform to social norms and standards, to avoid being ostracized by the herd.

The human brain is also hardwired to want to seek a mate in order to pass on genes. Finding someone who wants to be with you is of utmost importance to your brain. When you experience romantic rejection, you are naturally hurt because your chances of passing on your genes are challenged. This can also be very alarming and painful for the brain and it explains why romantic rejection is so painful and humiliating.

Now, life is still very difficult without the support of others. But it is not as impossible to survive on your own as it once was. The terror of being alone is still very much alive in humans, however. The hardwiring of the brain has not changed. The human brain has evolved very slowly, and society has evolved very quickly. The brain has not had time to catch up with new social changes. Therefore, the brain continues to hold onto old instincts that no longer serve people properly.

As a result, humans usually live with the natural and deep-seated pain of rejection as a residue from ancient history. Fear of rejection is an integral part of all people. It is hard for people to cope with the pain of rejection, so they naturally want to avoid it. However, avoiding rejection is not always possible. Rejection continues to hurt us but it is also an unfortunate part of daily life. In business and in romance, rejection occurs frequently. It is unavoidable, unless you want to stay in your house all day, never doing anything.

Unfortunately, much of the pain of rejection is self-inflicted. While rejection itself hurts, it actually becomes unbearable when someone ruminates on the rejection and begins to let it hurt their ego and make them question themselves. The sensation of rejection is so powerful that it can shake a person's very sense of belonging, leading to overly critical self-hatred. Not feeling like a part of the herd can make someone start to question their worth as a human being. The sense of being rejected can cause severe ego bruising. Many people begin to act self-destructively and worsen their pain by taking rejection too seriously, thinking that a single rejection reflects everything wrong within themselves.

Rejection tends to make people think of their own insecurities. If someone carries a great deal of insecurity, the first thing they think when they are rejected is that they are somehow too flawed to be accepted by others. As they attempt to find out what they did wrong to lead to the rejection so that they can adjust their behavior to conform, often they think of their own insecurities as the cause of the rejection. "I was rejected because I'm fat." "I am too pushy for anyone to love me." "I am not really a good painter, so that's why no one wants to carry my paintings in their galleries." Even if these are not the reasons behind rejection, people often blame their self-appointed flaws for their rejections. This just makes rejection hurt all the more, since people let rejection rub their most sensitive points.

Insecurities are often started at an early age. Perhaps they were planted in someone's brain by an abusive parent or peer, or they were learned through media. Regardless of how insecurities start, they can drive a person crazy. People often notice their flaws far more than others do. Rejection can make those flaws seem even worse. A rejection based on someone's flaw, such as a romantic rejection over weight, offers positive reinforcement for the insecurity, suggesting that it is a real flaw and really does prevent someone from being loved and accepted by others. In this way, rejection can deepen insecurities.

Rejection causes a feeling just like physical pain. But it also causes bursts of rage and mood disturbances. A large amount of rejection can result in long-term mood disturbance, such as depression. Focusing on things like your insecurities during rejection can only worsen the mental havoc of it.

Psychopaths like Ted Bundy are examples of people who let rejection drive them insane. They act on the spurts of rage and hurt that rejection can cause. Instead of licking their wounds alone at home until they heal, these people tend to react violently and forcefully. This extreme overreaction to rejection is just an example of how horribly and deeply rejection can hurt people. While most people do not act on the feelings that arise over rejection, rejection does elicit very powerful feelings and even violent thoughts.

Rejection over time can have two effects on a person. It can either harden someone against rejection and make them rejection-proof, or it can make someone fearful and reticent to really live life. How rejection affects you is really up to you. You can determine which way you want to let your brain handle rejection. But it is undoubtedly better if you choose to let rejection shape you into a stronger person. Turning the negative experience of rejection into a positive one can make you feel better and can make you become a pro at overcoming rejection in the future.

It is possible for you to choose how you want to look at rejection. Despite the power of instincts, you have an ability to retrain your brain to ignore your instincts when it comes to rejection. You can condition yourself against the fear of rejection, and you can teach yourself to embrace rejection as a learning experience by forcing yourself to have a positive attitude about it. You can also teach your brain to cease self-inflicting pain on yourself.

In time, by forcing a good attitude and ignoring your fear of rejection, you can train your brain to automatically look at rejection differently than it normally would. Your brain may naturally be inclined to shrink away from rejection in fear, but you can conquer the power of your instincts and train your brain to handle rejection as less than life-shattering. At first you will have to force your cheer, but in time, it will become a habit and your brain will automatically approach rejection without terror. When you achieve this level of understanding, you can begin to tackle life, unimpeded and unlimited by fear of the pain of rejection.

Take a lesson from author Jia Jiang. Jiang embarked on a mission to be rejected for a hundred days. Instead of letting a hundred rejections take away his zest for life, Jiang instead became determined to hear no. He shed all fear of rejection and dedicated himself to handling it well. He used rejection as means to explore himself as a person, and to become conditioned to rejection so that he could overcome it better in the future.

You do not have to deliberately seek out rejection for a hundred days, but you may find it very useful to use rejection as a means for learning how to avoid rejection in the future. Let rejection strengthen you and build you up, not weaken you and tear you down.

It all comes down to how you look at rejection. This is the topic of the next chapter.

Chapter 2: Change the Way You Look at Rejection

The first step to overcoming your fear of rejection is to change how you look at rejection. Changing your perspective on rejection can make it less daunting and terrifying to you. You can literally train your brain to stop halting at the fear of rejection, even though this fear is instinctual and ingrained in all human beings. Then, you will be able to conquer your fear and take the risks that make life happen. You will be amazed at how much you can accomplish in life when you do not let fear stop you from taking action.

By changing the way you look at rejection, you can change your relationship with rejection from one of fear to one of positive acceptance. Positive acceptance means that you accept rejection as a part of reality and you know that you cannot fight it. It also means that you begin to approach rejection from a solution-oriented angle, where you can work on solving rejection and the problems it causes, rather than running from it. With this better relationship with rejection, rejection stops being a barrier in your life. Instead, it becomes a mere facet of life that you are able to work through. The fear of rejection is replaced by problem-solving and innovation. This forms your road to success.

Accept Rejection

Rejection will happen in life. You can never be immune to it so you need to learn how to deal with it. Accepting the reality of rejection is crucial to overcoming your fear of it.

Unfortunately, you will not be everyone's cup of tea. There will be people who dislike you. There will be people who do not see value in what you have to offer, and who will turn you down in business or romance. Rejection is especially strong in certain fields, such as when you are starting up a business and trying to find investors or when you are trying to market a book, music, or other creative venture. You give something your best, but other people do not seem to find any value in it.

This hurts, but it is to be expected. It is also to be expected when you approach people that you find attractive. It does not mean that you are a terrible person or a loser that no one likes. Rather, it is because you are facing so much competition in the world. You must understand that rejection is the human response to inundation. With too many offers flooding in from all sides, people are required to be selective about where they put their resources and energy. They cannot dedicate time to everyone. Therefore, people are going to reject a good number of the offers that they receive. Just because you are rejected does not mean that you are worthless. You just happened to approach someone who could not see your value, for a reason that is beyond your control.

Rejection is likely to happen at least once in your life. But there is also a chance that you will be accepted, too. When you begin to fear rejection, think, "There is a fifty-fifty chance that

I will be rejected or accepted. If I do not try, I never find out which one it will be. I might as well try."

When you approach risks with this attitude, you remove yourself from feeling the fear that rejection inspires in most people. Accepting the fact that rejection will happen can help you prepare for it. You can develop a Plan B. Rejection is not the end of the world for you if you take the time to think of alternative options. It is always a great idea to think of what you will do should you be rejected. Accepting rejection allows you to begin thinking of solutions to rejection.

If you accept the possibility that rejection will occur, you will not be as surprised by it. The element of surprise is what can especially crumble your ego. You believe that something will happen, and when it does not, you have a long fall from your emotional high of confidence. But if you walk into something expecting a possible rejection, you will not be as crushed by surprise because you will not feel foolish when your certainty of acceptance proves to be false.

Consider All Possible Outcomes

It is possible for you to never want to take a chance because you see only one outcome: a hard no. But no matter how well you think you know someone, you cannot read minds. There are other possible outcomes than just a hard no.

Consider the different possibilities there are. You could hear a yes. You could hear a maybe. You could hear a no.

Next, you should consider how to react to each possible response. If you hear a maybe, you can start to really sell yourself to turn that maybe into a yes. On the other hand, you can think of an alternative plan if you hear a no. But what if you hear a yes? Then you need to start preparing for greatness!

Considering all the different outcomes to your proposal can create a fun sense of suspense. With this suspense, you can actually look forward to finding out what will happen when you take a chance. This can help motivate you to want to try something without as much fear.

View Rejection as Progression

A very helpful blog about rejection, called "Dumb Little Man," offers the mantra: View rejection as progression. This is great advice. You can develop an attitude that transforms something negative into a positive. Obviously rejection hurts, but instead of drowning in the pain, you can begin to feel better more quickly with a positive adjustment to your thinking.

Many people view rejection as regression. It is easy to believe that you work for a yes and then when you receive a no, all your efforts are wasted and you have to return to the beginning. This can certainly feel like regression.

But rejection is not taking a few steps backward. Rather, rejection means that you just took a step forward. Rejection is actually progress forward in life. Viewing rejection this way helps remove some of the pain from rejection.

Rejection is a forward movement in your life because you actually made the progress to presenting someone with your idea or proposal. You made it far enough to overcome your fear of rejection. Just because your idea was ultimately shot down does not discount the fact that you actually tried.

Rejection is also progression because it can teach you lessons and help you grow as a person. Every time you experience a rejection, you learn a bit about what does not work. You learn ways that you can improve what you are offering. You can find blind spots and oversights in your plans with the help of others.

Sometimes, a plan or idea seems perfect until you present it to someone who points out flaws that you never noticed. Similarly, when someone criticizes you as a person, you can start to learn things about yourself that you may need to change. While seeing the flaws in your work is painful, it also allows you to see what you can improve.

You should not base your life on or change yourself because of the opinions of others. But you can use the opinions of others to gain some insight into ways that you can improve yourself and your projects. Sometimes, you do not have the same perspective of yourself and your work that others do. Other people can offer some powerful insight into what you can change.

Unfortunately, hearing that you are not perfect can really hurt. But you can minimize the pain by using the negative input of others to improve yourself, rather than beat yourself down.

Don't Take It Personally

You should not take every rejection personally. Sometimes, rejection happens for reasons that have nothing to do with you. You yourself are not responsible for every rejection that you receive.

Sometimes people have other circumstances in their lives that prevent them from saying yes. A hot woman that you approach could be married or she could be too shy to talk to you. A business prospect who turns down your collaboration attempt may be struggling financially behind closed doors and cannot afford to collaborate with you. A publisher who sends you a rejection letter may not be able to publish any more books for that fiscal quarter, or the publishing company specializes in a different genre than the book you wrote.

Do not ever assume that rejection is based only on your flaws as a human being. Just because someone rejects you or your work does not mean that you have nothing valuable to offer the world. The rejection most likely speaks on them, not on you. There are a million reasons why someone may reject you, so don't take it personally and assume that the rejection is specifically because of you. You can save yourself a lot of heartache if you stop looking at rejection as a personal attack.

Rejection Is Not Always Because of Your Flaws

In the first chapter, I talked about how rejection often hurts because people beat themselves up over it. Most of the pain of rejection is self-inflicted. This self-inflicted pain comes from the human habit of translating rejection into some sort of statement about internal flaws. People tend to search for explanations about why they were rejected, leading them to imagining the causes of rejection. Often, people think of their insecurities as real, and they often assume that rejection occurred because of some flaw that they see inside themselves.

It is a mistake to make this assumption. You are not a mind reader, so do not attempt to read the minds of people who reject you. You can never know exactly what causes rejection unless someone tells you outright. Therefore, you cannot be sure that your deepest insecurities are responsible.

Usually only you can see the things that you are insecure about. You blow up tiny flaws, possibly even imagining flaws that are not even there. As a result, you think that you have deep, glaring flaws, and no one else does. Your self-magnified flaws are quite possibly NOT the cause of any rejection that you experience.

If you stop thinking that rejection is always because of your self-magnified flaws, you can seriously cut down on how much rejection hurts.

Rejection Now Doesn't Mean Rejection Later

One rejection, or even many rejections, does not mean that you will be rejected forever. The number of rejections you receive do not lower the fifty percent likelihood that you will be accepted in every future venture. If you try again, you may just succeed.

Many authors experience hundreds of rejections before finally getting their big break. Even the most famous actors sometimes struggled for years to get an important role. Everyone faces rejection. But perseverance is key. By not giving up, you may just find someone who will give you a yes rather than a no.

You need to keep going out and trying. Do not give into self-defeat over one rejection. Even several rejections do not mean that one day you will not be welcomed by someone with open arms. If you give up and start living in fear, you are standing the risk of missing out on that one special opportunity.

The day you give up on your dreams is the day that you start dying inside. Even if it seems that going on is pointless or even foolish, you cannot give up on what inspires you to feel passion for life. Your dreams are what give you the passion and joy to go on. Keep persevering and do not give up and miss out on what may just make your life wonderful.

This idea also applies to past rejections. You may have been rejected in the past and you now have trouble getting over it. Past rejections may have lowered your confidence and self-esteem, and created great fear in you that you cannot succeed in a certain venture. But the rejections of the past have no bearing on the future. You may just get a yes in the future. So work hard to overcome the past and stop letting past rejections hold you back. What was a no in the past may just be a yes in the future.

Find an Alternative

Sometimes, you get stuck on a certain track. You are determined to meet a goal or do things a certain way. This level of stubbornness can actually be a great quality. It can mean that you are great at perseverance. You should not give up and change yourself at the slightest rejection. Therefore, sticking to your original plan is a great idea.

But sometimes, you do need to change your ways. No matter how hard you try, you are not able to fit into the world's view of how you should be. An unorthodox business idea or project that does not fit into a normal genre may be great, but they may be hard to market to more traditional people. You may find that changing your plans can bring you more success.

It is not always fun to realize that you need to change. You think that you are on a good track, and finding out that you are not is heartbreaking. It can also be confusing to know how to reevaluate and change your plan. Just understand that changing your plans and your direction does not equal giving up. Pride can prevent you from admitting that you need to employ a different tactic, but you should not let pride keep you from making some better decisions for your life or your business.

It is possible that all you need to do is change your presentation. The way you present a business proposal or the way you approach an attractive person is how you make a first impression. We all know that bad first impressions are bad for you. Perhaps there is nothing wrong with your proposal, but your presentation fails to sell your proposal successfully. Sometimes all you need to do is tweak your presentation to make your proposal look more inviting and positive. Then, you are likely to experience more luck.

On the other hand, you may find that you have to change your actual proposal. It is not the presentation that is wrong, but instead you are offering people something that they are not interested in. You have to backtrack and find a new direction to take your proposal in. You may need to adjust your proposal to factor in the local demographic or to include trends that are popular right now to make it more marketable. You may find that you need to work on yourself, including your appearance and your manners, to become more appealing to others.

Changing the direction you are taking your project in can mean that you find a different avenue for your dreams. For instance, if you are trying to get into modeling but you are overweight, you can either lose weight or you can try to do plus size modeling. If you are trying to publish a genre-bending book, consider using an indie publishing company or self-publishing and marketing through sites like Smashwords or Amazon. Or you may find that your business idea is great, but not for your specific area because it does not appeal to the area's demographics, so you need to open your business elsewhere or offer a slightly different appeal.

You may find that conventional approaches do not work for you. So go a more unique route. If you cannot seem to make something work, consider trying a different avenue or location. Instead of giving up, just find alternatives that can actually let you succeed. Do not keep running against a wall and experiencing rejection after rejection.

Rejection hurts, but it can be a good indicator of how you can improve your business or yourself for true success. Rejection is sometimes the guidance you need to find what you are supposed to do. View rejection as a valuable lesson and piece of guidance, rather than a punishment.

It is Just One Person's Opinion

With billions of people in the world, focusing on the opinion of just one person is foolish. You should not let one person tell you who you are. You cannot base your image of yourself on the opinion of just one person. Be aware that all people are different and the opinion of one person does not reflect the opinions of all people.

Often, people make the mistake of blowing someone up in their minds. They assign too much importance to one person's opinion. There are people in your life that you will want to impress. A boss, a parent, a friend, a prospective client or lover – the opinions of these people can mean a great deal to you. But sometimes you are only setting yourself up for heartbreak when you base all of your happiness on the opinion of one single person. You have every right to desire to impress someone, but if you fail to impress him or her, you are not worthless. You have no reason to let one person's opinion crush you or tell you who you are.

If someone rejects you, understand that their opinion is not necessarily fact. Just because someone does not find you to be good enough does not mean that you are not, in fact, good enough. Someone else may enjoy what you have to offer and may take you on. A rejection does not mean anything about who you are or what you have to offer. Rather, it says more about the person who rejected you than you.

Multiple rejections can start to make you really question your worth. When multiple people do not think you are good enough, you may start to wonder if you are. It may certainly seem like the majority vote is true. But you are not looking at a true majority vote. Again, since there are billions of people in the world, the opinions of a select few are not all-inclusive.

Running into a wall and facing multiple rejections often indicates that you are trying to do something new and dynamic. People often fear broadening their horizons. Your ideas or proposals may ask them to take risks that they are scared of taking. It does not mean that you are not offering anything of value to the world.

You simply are not reaching the right people with the same boldness and uniqueness as you. It is important to not doubt yourself or give up based on the opinions of a few fearful people. Rather, you should keep pressing on. You can even try using different angles or taking your work along different avenues. There is likely a niche for you, and you just have to find it.

Use It as Motivation to Sell Yourself

Rejection is the end for some people. But do not view it as an end to a deal. Rather, it could be the beginning. A no is not always solid. Rather, a no is an invitation for you to prove how deeply you really want something. If you actually are willing to push past the word no and start really selling yourself to change a no into a yes, you may just earn the respect of the people around you, especially the person who is rejecting you. You will prove that you are actually motivated and that you really want something. You will also become more desperate and start trying to sell yourself.

"The sale doesn't start until someone says no." This is a popular salesman's adage. When someone says no, that means that you really need to put effort into getting them to say yes. You can begin to sell yourself and your idea or project with even greater fervor.

Many people look at no as a permanent answer. But go-getters look at no as just a beginning in the negotiation process. Instead of taking no for an answer, take no as an inspiration to try harder. Let rejection motivate you rather than drag you down.

A No Won't Kill You

The most important aspect of rejection-proofing yourself is reminding yourself that rejection is not the end of the world. Because of evolutionary instinct, the human brain is programmed to blow rejection up into the worst thing that could possibly happen. But in our modern society, being rejected from the herd does not result in your immediate death at the jaws of some wild animal. You are able to survive rejection and move on.

Think back on the rejections you have experienced throughout your life. All of these rejections probably hurt at some level. Some probably hurt enough that they felt like the end. Your ego may have been crushed and your confidence smashed to smithereens. But you are still alive. You made it through those trying and hurtful rejections ultimately unscathed.

Therefore, you will make it through any future rejections, too. Again, it will probably hurt. There is no use lying and saying that rejection does not hurt. But if you are rejected in any venture, you are going to survive. You just have to pick up the pieces and move on. Do not let fear of something that does not really end your life keep you from living fully and taking chances.

Chapter 3: How to Handle Rejection Like a Pro

In the previous chapter, I talked about how you need to expect rejection in life and accept it as a part of reality. When rejection happens to you, you do not have to let it destroy your ego or your life's work. Rather, you can learn to handle the often painful event of rejection like a pro. You can move forward with your life and stop drowning in the pain and the fear by using some simple coping mechanisms.

Obviously, the first step to handling rejection well is changing how you look at rejection, using the tips included in Chapter 2. A better attitude about rejection helps you overcome your fear of it, but it also sets you up to handle rejection better should it actually happen. A better mental attitude about rejection prepares you to accept rejection and approach it as a way to improve yourself or your business proposal or craft. You will no longer view rejection as the end of the road, but rather the beginning of a new road. Holding this view can make you handle rejection in a manner that is more conducive to solutions and better for your ego.

Even with a good attitude about rejection, rejection still hurts. You can work to overcome the pain by viewing rejection as a chance to improve yourself, rather than a direct assault on your emotions and your ego. You can dedicate your mental energy to finding new ways to get accepted, rather than dwelling on the emotional sting of being rejected.

Make It a Learning Experience

Rejection is usually a negative experience. But you can ease the pain of this negative experience by emphasizing the few positives within the experience. Look on the bright side and analyze a rejection for all of the positives that it can bring you, rather than the negatives.

You may ask, "What could be positive about rejection? I just got shot down! What could make me happy about this?"

The main positive about rejection is that it offers you a chance to learn something. You can learn a lot about other people, yourself, and your work when you experience rejection. Rejection does point out that something you did was not good enough, which hurts. But it can also offer you insight into how to make your project good enough later on.

Some people are just rude and will reject you without offering any feedback. But some people are very helpful and offer constructive criticism along with their rejection. If someone offers you constructive criticism, put your ego aside and really listen. There may be some value to what someone is telling you. You can use this constructive criticism to correct any issues or downsides to your work.

Sometimes listening to your gut is all you need to improve yourself. If you get shot down and you think you know why, you should not assume that your insecurities are the root cause of your rejection. But if you are positive that something you feel insecure about led to the rejection, then perhaps your gut is telling you something valuable. Perhaps you already know that there is something wrong, and your gut is nagging at you to fix it. Listen to your gut and improve anything that you feel is not up to par to your standards, and the standards of your peers. In Chapter 2, I advised you not to blame your insecurities for rejection. While this is sound advice, you can also listen to your insecurities for clues on how to improve yourself. Often, your insecurities offer insight into things that you want to change about yourself. If you change the things that you hate about yourself, you may just fix what is causing others to reject you. You are doing this for yourself more than other people. Even if you do not change how the world perceives you, you will at least feel more confident and this can aid you in selling yourself or your product or idea with greater gusto. You will undoubtedly be more appealing and experience greater success if you feel more confident about yourself and project less insecurity.

If you cannot figure out why exactly you were rejected and your gut does not shed any additional light on the matter, then you should do your best to learn about how to be successful. Try studying how other more successful people do things. For instance, if you seem to always be rejected when you write proposals, try looking at samples of winning proposals from other professionals. You may gain some enlightenment on better ways to write a proposal that will get you a yes. In another example, perhaps you want to get a job in a certain field but you keep getting rejected because you have no work experience. You can make up for your lack of experience by studying the field you are trying to break into and becoming more knowledgeable so that you look like a worthwhile candidate for the position you are going for. Do not be afraid to study and learn all that you can about a subject. Your knowledge and your subsequent confidence on the material will make you shine as a stellar candidate.

Use rejection as a motivation to learn the most that you can. Study and look at examples to gain the experience and knowledge you need to be a better candidate for a job or a collaboration. Rejection can be your cue to become more educated and prepared.

Rejection can teach you some hard lessons about what people want and like. These lessons can help you become more marketable in the future. You learn what works in a presentation and what does not. You learn how to be more appealing. Rejection is basically a tough love lesson in how to be more efficient and marketable in business, creativity, and even romance. For instance, you may learn that breathing down someone's neck is not way to come across as an appealing romantic partner. Rather, being suave and offering to buy someone a drink usually works much better.

View it as Someone's Loss

When you are rejected, it can be helpful to understand that is someone else's loss, more than yours. You should have confidence that you offer something great. If someone turns you down, then he or she is the one suffering. You can just take your great ideas somewhere else, and let someone else benefit from working with you.

Imagine how the people who rejected J.K. Rowling feel now. J.K. Rowling experienced hundreds of rejections for her first Harry Potter novel. Now, she is richer than the Queen of England and Harry Potter has become an internationally acclaimed franchise and a household name. Everyone knows who the child wizard is and almost everyone has read the books and/or seen the movies. The agents who rejected J.K. Rowling really missed out when they refused to represent her novel.

The people who reject you now are also going to miss out. Your book or whatever you are trying to market can be the next biggest craze. You stand to make a fortune in the future, as will anybody who gives you a chance. The people who rejected you are the ones who will regret doing so in the future, as they miss out on millions of dollars and plenty of fame. They did not believe in you and as a result, they do not get to soar to the heights of fame and fortune with you.

Often, people utter the phrase, "Your loss" as a shallow attempt to gain false comfort. But you do not have to reap only false comfort from this belief. You can genuinely make yourself feel better and continue to believe in the value of what you are offering the world if you view the people who reject you as fools that are missing out on something great. Move on and find someone who really does appreciate what you have to offer. The people who reject you just made a big mistake!

Find New Reasons to Live

You should not base all of your happiness on one thing. If you do, you will likely find yourself disappointed again and again. If you try to accomplish something and you get rejected, you do not have to feel like you have failed your life purpose. There are other things out there for you to live for.

You should never give up on a dream. But if you do decide that a dream is impossible, then you should not give up on living a great life altogether. Instead, begin to find new dreams and goals. Do not settle for less. Keep aspiring to greatness and trying to accomplish everything that you set your heart to. There is so much to do and be in the world, that you should not let yourself die inside with the unsuccessful conclusion of one venture.

You should shift your focus from the person or group that rejected you. Instead, find new people to focus on who actually want to work with you or be with you. Focus on old or new hobbies. Focus on bringing old dreams back to the surface. It is a great idea to shift focus from rejection and start to find a new zest for life.

Rejection can actually be the push you need to start living a more fulfilling life. If something does not work out, you now have the opportunity to try new ventures. You can adjust your focus to more beneficial, fruitful things.

You are the Harbinger of Your Own Destiny

There are two forms of control over your destiny, external and internal. External control are forces outside of you that influence your happiness and your moods and thoughts. Internal forces are the attitudes, beliefs, and thoughts within your own mind that influence your destiny.

Rejection is usually an external force that can make you feel like you have lost control. When you approach someone, you put part of your destiny in their hands. If they reject you, it can feel as if they are a huge, monstrous force, much like a hurricane, ruining your life. You feel like you are at the mercy of an external force, and this can make you feel powerless and battered. You may even feel like you have terrible luck. As you give up on the external forces around you, you begin to give up on yourself because you no longer see how much power you really do hold over your own life.

It is important to take that power back into your own hands. Do not feel like you are somehow worthless because an external force worked against you. After all, you are the harbinger of your own destiny. You can give up power, or you can take it back. Taking hold of your own power can make you feel more powerful and can lead to greater success in your life.

Just because someone rejects you does not mean that you are powerless and at the mercy of others. You may feel that way, especially in business when you rely on clients and investors for your survival, but really, you are the one who is in control. You are the one offering people something great. You can seize that control and begin to rejection-proof yourself. You can make your idea or product even more valuable with some necessary tweaks. You can approach different avenues.

Do not give up control over your life or your destiny. Your internal forces can have great influence over your external forces. By thinking positively and taking the initiative, you can begin to regain control over your life and your chances of success.

Chapter 4: Get Rejected Less

You cannot always avoid rejection, but you can make yourself more appealing so that you experience much less rejection. With a few relatively simple tactics, you can influence others and external forces around you to embrace you rather than push you away. Your chances of being rejected or accepted are still technically fifty-fifty in all situations, but you can tip the odds in your favor by projecting confidence and presenting yourself and your proposals in a more appealing way.

Offer People What They Like

Understanding what appeals to people is an important part of becoming more acceptable. All people are different and unique in what they look for in others. Therefore, there are no set rules in what works for everyone. It is necessary to read people and get to know them quickly so that you can determine how to appeal to them. Find out what they like, and then tailor your proposal to match their desires while avoiding their dislikes.

You need to become adept at reading people. If a man dresses nicely, it is probably best to dress nicely when approaching him. If a woman wears a certain floral perfume, you can gather that she likes that type of scent and you can attempt to woo her with gifts that smell similar to her perfume.

You can also gather clues about what people want by really listening to them when they talk. Do they mention that they have a family? If so, they probably want family time, vacation time, money, and financial stability. Do they mention that they hate being hassled during lunch? If so, find out their lunch hour and avoid calling or texting during that time.

Also consider the culture that someone is from. If they are from a foreign culture, consider researching mannerisms from their country of origin to determine how to come across the most appealing. For instance, appearing tall can make you seem important, which is often appealing to people in America, but not in other countries, such as Asian countries. So you should wear high heels or other heightening shoes when meeting an American, and flats when meeting someone with an Asian background. Learn about appropriate signs of respect and greetings, as well. Not all countries love firm handshakes and people who speak first.

When it comes to business, presentation can be everything. You need to present your proposal in a way that appeals to the people who are calling the shots. Make sure that your proposal offers them what you know they want. Also, consider the field you are going into so that you can adjust your presentation to match their standards. If you are entering a more creative field, consider making your presentation or resume artsy. If you are entering a more conservative field, leave off the frills. You can look at examples of resumes and presentations for different professional fields to get an idea of what you should do. The more appealing your presentation and proposal is, the more likely it is to be accepted.

While people are indeed unique, there are some things that all people like and appreciate. For instance, dressing nicely and being on time for a meeting, job interview, or date is a basic expectation of you that everyone shares. Good-smelling breath is also welcomed by all. When you are presenting something, it is best to be clear to avoid confusion, which can turn off people, especially busy people. Some people are more lenient than others, but it is best to never try your luck. Always be respectful, polite, clear, well-dressed, and well-groomed when approaching others. You can increase your luck by appealing to people with politeness, good hygiene, great presentation, and a professional image.

Focus on Them, Not You

When you are trying to appeal to someone, is important to always focus on how others will benefit from working with you or dating you. Do not make this about you or how much you need something. Others often do not and cannot care about what you want. Rather, you need to spin this to be all about them. Present only benefits and make your offer especially tempting. Make them feel like by accepting you, they are purchasing a ticket to paradise and solving all of their problems.

Salespeople are masters at this. They know how to sell a product by making you feel like the product is going to make your life perfect. Follow this lead and really sell yourself. Make yourself seem like the answer to someone's prayers. Do not be shy or modest, as this is not the time. Being bold and confident is key to making people feel like you are worth considering as a candidate.

Project Confidence

When you project confidence, you inspire others to be confident in you. Confidence can make you very appealing and can make people strongly consider accepting whatever you are proposing.

There are many ways to appear confident, even you are not feeling so bold on the inside. One of the ways is how you carry yourself. When you approach someone, keep a bold posture, with your spine straight and your chest out. Always keep eye contact to show that you have nothing to hide and nothing to be ashamed of. Give firm handshakes. Speak as if you know what you are talking about. Avoid stammering and stuttering and using placeholder words like "um," as these things can make you seem nervous. Try to use a broader vocabulary to show how smart you are, but of course make sure you only use words that you actually know the meanings of. Nothing can make you look like a bigger idiot than if you are throwing around words in improper contexts.

Taking care of your appearance is also very important. By looking your best, you project the vibe that you care about yourself and have a decent amount of self-esteem. Frumpy people are unattractive because they do not appear to respect themselves or care about themselves. You want to try to make an effort to look and smell good. Dress to impress.

Talk like the Deal is Already in the Bag

One way to influence people is to make them feel like a deal is already made. This makes people feel like they are unable to reject you. Talking like the deal is already in the bag is a popular sales tactic. It puts pressure on people to say yes because they feel like everything is already decided and it would be wrong for them to say no.

Avoid Appearing Alone

In a social experiment, a young man entered a strange bar alone and began talking to women. Usually he had pretty good luck with women in the bar he usually went to where he knew everyone, but when he approached the women in this bar, he did not have luck at all. Some of the women even tossed drinks in his face.

Later, he went back to the same bar, but with a group of guy friends. They laughed and bought beers and played darts. Within just an hour of being in the bar, the young man noticed that women were looking at him with interest. When he approached women, he found that he had his luck back.

This experiment illustrates how important it is to appear like you have friends in the world.

By appearing to be liked by others, you can make people feel like they can like you too. This is because of the natural herd instinct that people possess. When you have friends, this leads others to want to follow suit and make friends with you, too. It shows the world that you are likable and a part of the human herd.

When you are trying to avoid rejection, use your friends and connections to make yourself seem more likable. Get endorsements. Show that others found you worth accepting. This can influence someone to feel like it is a good idea to accept you, too.

Be Persistent

Persistence wins the race. You need to be persistent, almost to the point of being annoying.

Use persistence to doggedly get what you want. You are more likely to get your way if you persevere and never give up.

Persistence shows how much you care and how dedicated you are to something. If you show someone how badly you want it, they may be more willing to trust you with a chance.

Persistence always keeps you in the race. You do not give up, so you do not have a chance to miss out. You continue to try until your opportunity comes along.

You also can pester people into finally giving in, just to get rid of you. But this kind of persistence can be risky. If you annoy someone too much, you may lose their interest forever. You want to be persistent and bold without being rude. Do not call at inappropriate times or more than once a day, for instance.

Be Emotionally Detached

Emotional detachment can lead to carelessness. But it is not always a bad thing. In fact, it is advisable when you are opening yourself up for possible rejection. Emotionally detach yourself from the things that are important to you so that you can appear more confident and feel less crushed by possible rejection.

Do not confuse emotional detachment with not caring. Being emotionally detached from your work or other areas of life does not mean that you do not care. You really should care. But you do not have to invest all of your happiness into something. You also should not base your life and your sense of success on it. Do not make the mistake of thinking that one accomplishment, one yes, will solve all of your problems and send you on a magical path to forever happiness.

Emotional detachment is more likely to help you appear confident, rather than desperate. People prefer confidence over desperation, so emotional detachment can serve you well in the long run. Avoid projecting any type of desperation to get an acceptance. Desperation can make you appear badly to the people that you are trying to sell yourself to. Stop feeling like an acceptance is a dire need and a rejection would be the end of the world. Have other things in your life that you can fall back on, and alternative courses of action. This is how you can become emotionally detached from your work and appear more confident. Your confidence will be genuine if you have a fallback option and do not depend entirely upon someone's approval.

There is an additional benefit to emotionally removing yourself from things. When you are emotionally detached, rejection is less likely to crush you. Rejection comes as a part of life and you can brush it off and move on. Being emotionally detached allows you to be persistent and to not retreat into a hole of fear because of your wounded ego.

Chapter 5: Different Types of Rejection

Rejection can occur in all areas of life. You may experience rejection in your personal or professional life. You may encounter it at work, at school, or even at home with your own family. The way rejection affects you can vary based on the context, but it always hurts. You can learn different ways to handle rejection specific to certain areas of your life, however, to minimize the pain.

Romantic Rejection

Romantic rejection can hurt more than all other rejection. A break-up or hearing a "no" when you ask someone out or propose to someone can really lower your self-esteem. You have to deal with a slew of emotions, ranging from anger to confusion to self-doubt to grief. Often, it can take a long while to begin to overcome a romantic rejection of any kind.

Sometimes, a romantic rejection feels equivalent to suffering withdrawals from a drug. This is because love releases hormones such as serotonin and testosterone and oxytocin. These hormones are feel-good hormones and the sudden stopping of them can create a type of physical withdrawal. MRIs have revealed that the same part of brain that activates during cocaine withdrawal also activates during romantic rejection.

In addition, couples often share joint memories. When you lose a partner that you have been close to for a while, you lose part of your memories. This is why a break-up can feel like losing a part of yourself. These two aspects of love can make a sudden rejection hurt especially badly.

Previous emotional wounds can also reopen at the event of a rejection, because you are reminded of the past. Previous wounds only add to your pain and your ego bruising.

It is important to not let romantic rejection make you stop trying to find true love. Even if you have experience multiple rejections throughout the course of your life, this does not mean that you are destined to be alone until you die. Often, people give up and grow bitter when they experience failure. But failure in love is often not your fault. Romantic rejection usually speaks more about the person that rejected you, rather than you. You can overcome romantic rejection by realizing that it is not all of your fault and that you can move on and find someone better. Really, if someone rejects you, you should consider it a sign that that person is not good enough for you, instead of thinking that you are not good enough.

If a break-up was clearly your fault, use it as a learning experience. There are other people out there who deserve your very best treatment. You can use your failed relationships to learn how to become better to the person you date in the future.

You can also use rejection as a way to learn how to improve your flirting technique. If you consistently get turned down, consider it a sign that your technique needs to be upgraded.

Begin developing your social skills and working on how you look.

When you are suffering through a break-up, think about the bad things. Your entire relationship was probably littered with warning signs that it was not meant to be. Think about your ex and his or her flaws. It is highly unlikely that he or she is perfect. With time, you can begin to realize that you two were not meant to be and not perfect for each other. You can free yourself from regret and self-doubt and move on, knowing that it was not your fault that you were rejected.

Social Rejection

The natural human need to be accepted as part of the herd is what makes social rejection so hard. Not fitting in and being excluded by other people can trigger the parts of the brain that associates rejection with possible death. It is not a good feeling.

There are many possible reasons for social rejection. You may be ostracized by society for your lifestyle choices. You may be socially awkward and cannot converse with people easily. You may have a disability, mental illness, or other problem that is beyond your control, but earns you disgust and rejection from others. You may have made a mistake in your past or you may have been accused of a crime that makes even your loved ones turn against you. Deviating from social standards in any way can make you become an object of rejection. No matter why you are rejected socially, it is not your fault. But you must endure constant humiliation and pain every time someone rejects you.

The pain of social rejection can drive you to isolate yourself in order to stop experiencing the pain. You let fear overtake your life and you live in loneliness because you are too afraid to keep putting yourself out there. Alternatively, you may strive to become someone that you are not. You try your hardest to fit in and deny parts of who you are just so that you appear socially acceptable. Not only do your efforts often prove useless, but you also become incredibly unhappy and insecure. The people who do love you for you are often put off by your fake persona and you begin to experience more rejection than you did while being your unique self.

Social rejection hurts. But it is not a good reason to change yourself into someone you are not or to live in isolation. You do not need to give up on having a social life. You just need to find your niche. Finding your niche calls for you to be true to yourself, so that you can attract like people.

You should also never change yourself. It is important to remember that there is nothing and no one just like you. You are unique. It would be a shame to change your uniqueness in any way, especially for other people. Other people are not worth your happiness or your security. Usually, the people whose opinions you care about are not worthy of your attention. They do not pay your bills, uplift you, or add any other sort of value to your life. So why should you dedicate so much emotional energy to them? Let go of these people. And do not ever change yourself for them.

Creative Rejection

One of the areas in life where people experience the most rejection is in creative pursuits. If you are an artist or inventor of any sort, you know how it feels to pour all of your energy and all of your ego into a project. You can spend days, months, and even years perfecting a masterpiece. When you complete your project, you feel that it is beautiful and you cannot wait to show it to the world. Yet for some reason, other people are blind to the beauty and depth of your work. They do not understand or appreciate your work. Most likely, they also value work that you feel is beneath yours. The lack of appreciation other people show your work can make you start to question the true value of your project, and can crumble your ego.

Art takes a certain amount of confidence and ego. You must believe in your work to pursue it. You would not keep putting time and effort into something that you believe is ugly and worthless. Therefore, you invest a large amount of your pride in your work and you believe that your work is worthy of praise. Rejection is often a harsh blow because it dismantles your belief in yourself and your work.

Unfortunately, criticism and rejection in the world of art is inevitable. Competition also runs high. Often, the esteem certain artists garnish is based on their connections, not the quality of their work. This is unfair but it is reality. Keep this in mind when you feel the bitter sting of jealousy. Your work is not subpar. It just is not as highly publicized.

People also have different taste. It is very possible that people out there will not like your work. That does not mean that no one does. Some people may love your work. You have to keep trying and putting yourself out there, until you finally reach your target audience. The more you show off your art, the more people you reach. Do not let a few naysayers make you feel like no one will ever like your work.

Focus more on your enjoyment of artistry than pleasing people. Your confidence will reflect in your presentation and in your work. It can actually have the unintended effect of making people become your fans.

Business Rejection

Trying to get investors, grants, clients, customers, or even public awareness for your business requires you to put yourself out there. This opens you up to rejection. Rejection is highly likely, especially in business, when money is involved. People are picky about where they place their money and so they are extremely selective about business transactions and investments.

Marketing is the key to overcoming business-related rejection. You must present your business proposal in a way that makes you appear worthwhile. Gaining an understanding of marketing is necessary for you to expand and sell yourself in the business world. While marketing basics lies beyond the scope of this book, there are a few basic premises of marketing that you should definitely know. The first is that you need to know who your demographic is so that you can determine how to best appeal to the people that are the most likely to buy your product. The second is that you must do market research to observe what other similar companies are doing. Finally, you need to present your research to investors and use your knowledge to create desirable marketing for your demographic.

Business rejection is an inevitable part of business life. But it should not affect your ego. The people who reject you are missing out on a potentially lucrative business. Just persevere, and understand that you can make your own success. Believe in yourself and your business.

Conclusion

Rejection is not pleasant for anyone. It denies your need to be loved and accepted by someone. But rejection is an unfortunate reality of life. You cannot let it limit you, or you will never risk anything and take your life further. You will keep yourself in a tight box of fear.

After the initial hurtful sting of rejection fades away, you need to get back up on your feet. Do not let the fear of pain keep you whimpering in a shell. You need to break out of your shell and take on life, with or without rejection.

Life is not meant to be lived in security. You can create a bubble for yourself, where you never take the risk of being rejected. But then you miss out on so many chances where you might be accepted. Your ideas and your dreams will never see the light of day if you remain closed off from the world in fear.

The pain of rejection is not worth the pain of a life of regrets. Take some of the big risks that make life go round. You will never know if something will work out better than you could have ever hoped unless you try.

With this book as your guide, you can start working on overcoming your fear of rejection. Stop living in fear and start living your life. If you have a business idea, a novel, a script, or someone that you want to ask out, go for it. You may just get a yes. And if you get a no, it is just a chance to grow and move on to the next great thing in your life. The rejection of one person does not reflect anything on you.

Someone else may welcome you or your ideas with open arms.

Fear of rejection should not hold you back. You should embrace life. Take risks. Try new things. Make yourself rejection-proof so that rejection just bounces off of you and does not stop you from truly living. The ideas in this book can help you become invincible, to where rejection does not stop you.

Other books available by Madison Taylor on Kindle, paperback and audio:

Cognitive Behavioral Therapy for Beginners: How to Use CBT to Overcome Anxieties, Phobias, Addictions, Depression, Negative Thoughts, and Other Problematic Disorders

References

Dumb Little Man. *How to Handle Rejection Like a Pro*. Retrieved from http://www.businessinsider.com/facing-rejection-here-are-5-key-steps-to-handle-them-like-a-pro-2011-5. 2011.

Jiang, Jia. *Rejection Proof: How I Beat Fear and Became Invincible Through 100 Days of Rejection*. Harmony Publishing: New York City, New York. 2015.